PUFFI

Mad

W

Cartoonist and comedy writer John Byrne has published many best-selling books for children and adults, although this is his first one for dogs. He lives in London with his wife and family and is very happy (you can tell that because of his shiny coat and wet nose!).

PUFFIN BOOKS

Published by the Penguin Group
Penguin Books Ltd, 27 Wrights Lane, London W8 5TZ, England
Penguin Putnam Inc., 375 Hudson Street, New York, New York 10014, USA
Penguin Books Australia Ltd, Ringwood, Victoria, Australia
Penguin Books Canada Ltd, 10 Alcorn Avenue, Toronto, Ontario, Canada M4V 3B2
Penguin Books (NZ) Ltd, Private Bag 102902, NSMC, Auckland, New Zealand

On the world wide web at: www.penguin.com

Penguin Books Ltd, Registered Offices: Harmondsworth, Middlesex, England

First published 1999
1 3 5 7 9 10 8 6 4 2

Made and printed in England by Clays Ltd, St Ives plc

British Library Cataloguing in Publication Data
A CIP catalogue record for this book is available from the British Library

ISBN 0–141–30043–4

MAD MAGS

WOOF!

John Byrne

PUFFIN BOOKS

Letter from the Editor

GOOD DOGGY!

You've sniffed out the latest copy of WOOF! magazine and now it's in your panting paws. No other magazine offers such a powerful pooch's-eye view of all that's going on in the wonderful world of woofness.

In this issue, our doggy readers can bone up on all the latest news, ferret out our fascinating features, and see which mongrel megastars our rover-ing reporters have been hounding for interviews. And of course there's our usual selection of exciting adverts guaranteed to make a dog's life all the doggier.

Pooches please note: If you picked up your copy of WOOF! while you were fetching your owner's newspaper, make sure YOU get to read it first. Yes, WOOF! is a hundred times more interesting than humanly possible but, after all, fair's fair. And not only that, fur's fur.

Now enough of my whining – I can tell you're straining at the leash to start chewing over the latest issue. Just don't chew too much of it or you won't have any room left for your steak dinner.

Rupert Mur-Dog
Editor

P.S. If you enjoyed this issue of WOOF!, or even if you didn't, please keep sending in all those great letters. I don't actually READ them, but they do make a lovely warm lining for the bottom of my basket.

What's In A Name?

You may have heard that human names have hidden meanings. Well, we at WOOF! have discovered that this applies to dogs, too. Now you can find out what your name really says about you!

Spot: Your owner was probably given you as a present after suffering from a nasty attack of chicken pox.

Prince: Every time your owner kisses you, you turn into a frog.

Fido: Your real name is 'Tiddles' but as you're a huge, musclebound watchdog, nobody thinks it's a good idea to mention it.

Rex: You're getting on a bit. And 'Tyrannosaurus' is too long a word to fit on the disc around your neck.

Fang: You're mean and nasty and like to bite people ... so it's lucky you've only got one tooth.

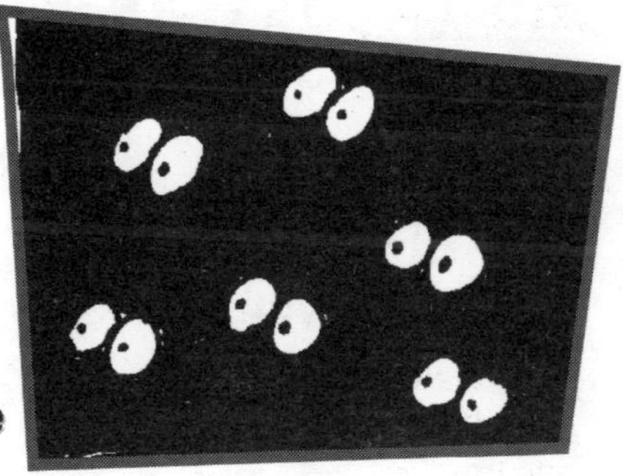

Lassie: Your owner likes to name pets after film stars. You probably live in the same house as a rabbit called Bugs, a piglet called Babe and a budgie called Arnold Schwarzenegger.

Rover: Your owner wanted a car instead.

OK OWNER

What sort of human do *you* live with? Check them out with this handy WOOF! guide ...

OK OWNERS take you for walks even when their favourite TV programme's on.

MOULDY MASTERS take you for walks when YOUR favourite programme's on.

OK OWNERS let you sleep on the bed because they love you.

MOULDY MASTERS let you sleep on the bed because they're too mean to buy a blanket.

OK OWNERS buy the yummiest dog food.

MOULDY MASTERS buy the yummiest dog food ... and then eat it all themselves.

OK OWNERS make sure you don't get fleas.

MOULDY MASTERS have more fleas than you in the first place.

or MOULDY MASTER?

K OWNERS tell their
eachers that you ate
heir homework.
OULDY MASTERS
ctually make you do
he homework for them.
(And you get more of
he answers right!)

OK OWNERS are a
dog's best friend.
MOULDY MASTERS need
to learn who's Top Dog
around here.

OK OWNERS don't always make you take a bath.
MOULDY MASTERS are so smelly, you have to make THEM take a bath.

Let's speak Human

Are you tired of humans lording it over you just because they think they're the *only* animals who can speak? They may be all talk – but YOU can be all talk too, with our simple language course.

When a human asks
"How do you feel this morning?"
simply say:
"RUFF!"

When a human asks
"What kind of animal went to sea with the pussycat?"
just reply:
"HOWL!"

And when a human yells **"Who made that big puddle on the front doorstep?"** SAY ABSOLUTELY NOTHING ... **Now you really are more clever than humanly possible.**

CANINE crossword

Many dogs have written in to WOOF! to complain that the clues in our weekly crossword are far too hard. So in order to please our loyal readers, we have put together a crossword which is so simple any dumb creature should be able to manage it.

Don't believe us?
Have a go yourself ...

■	■	■	1.	■
■	2.			
■		■		■
1.				■
■		■	■	■

ACROSS
1. What people who can't pronounce 'R' call a roof
2. 'FOOW' spelled backwards

DOWN
1. A shorter name for the World Organization Of Fish
2. The well-known alternative to 'Bark!'

ANSWERS: IF you REALLY need the answers to this puzzle, we've got some more crosswords for you. Unfortunately they're far too cross to repeat in a family magazine.

Fresh breath! Dazzling smile!

What dog in their right mind would want to put up with that?

Brush your teeth with Doggydent first thing in the morning and you can be sure that your dog breath will be absolutely diabolical throughout the whole day.

Available in both Three Week Old Sausage and Six Day Old Sock Flavours.

'You'll wonder where your friends all went when you brush your teeth with Doggydent!'

DOGGYDENT

Special Money Saving Offer:

Save your money – don't brush your teeth at all.

Continuing WOOF!'s series of in-depth interviews with dogs in unusual jobs, we invite you to meet:

Bonzo Baskerville: *Witch's Dog*

WOOF!: How did you get your job in the first place? Isn't it more usual for witches to have cats?
BB: My witch is allergic to cats. They bring her out in a horrible red rash. With me around she can still have her horrible green rash, same as usual.
WOOF!: Did you need to have any special training?
BB: Just the usual stuff like 'Heel', 'Stay','Beg'... although 'Sit' can be a bit difficult when you're on a broomstick flying through the air at 60 mph.
WOOF!: Is there anything dogs would normally do that your witch won't allow?
BB: Well, she does get a bit upset when I bury bones.
WOOF!: Why's that?
BB: Because Bones is a skeleton friend of hers and he gives her a real ear-bashing when she has to go out and dig him up again.
WOOF!: What's your favourite flavour of dog food?
BB: I can't make up my mind. Sometimes it's beef, or another time it might be chicken ... although when I'm working I'm quite partial to eye of newt and ear of bat.
WOOF!: So you don't think being a witch's dog makes you unusual at all?
BB: Certainly not. In fact I'll prove it. Throw that stick for me and I'll fetch it.
WOOF!: Okay. But this doesn't look like a stick to me. It looks more like a magic wa – OOPS!
BB: Ribit, Ribit!
WOOF!: Bonzo Baskerville, witch's ... er ... frog, thank you for talking to us.

WOOF!

Bonzo Baskerville: *Witch's Dog*

CANINE COOKERY

Don't be a peckish pooch. Here are some handy recipes guaranteed to fill the spot (or the Rover or the Fido or the Rex). We've graded the recipes in order of difficulty. (Of course if you're really hungry you may just decide to chew up the page itself.)

EASY RECIPE:

Big Juicy Bone

Ingredients: Map (We can't remember where we buried the big juicy bone)
One large shovel

FAIRLY EASY RECIPE:

Sausage and Mash

Ingredients: One dozen prime sausages
Several large potatoes
Butter
Herbs and spices

Step One: Mash potatoes in a mixing bowl.
Step Two: Add butter to make them creamy.
Step Three: Add herbs and spices to make them tasty.
Step Four: Chuck the whole lot out of the window. What dog's going to waste time eating mash when they could be scoffing all those sausages?

VERY EASY RECIPE:
Steak Surprise

Ingredients: Steak

Step One: Find out where your owner's left the steak.
Step Two: Scoff it.
Step Three: Won't they get a surprise!

EASIEST RECIPE OF ALL:
Large Tin of Dog Food

Ingredients:
Your voice

Just One Step:
Simply stand outside your owner's bedroom window and howl. Sooner or later they'll buy you a big tin of dog food just to shut you up.

Pet Owner PROBLEMS

Is your master driving you mad?
Does your mistress make mistakes?

Doctor Rex Rathbone

answers your queries

Dear Dr Rex

**Every time my owner comes near me he suffers terrible fits of sneezing.
What can I do?**

Fluffy, Fulham

Dear Fluffy,
Your owner is obviously allergic to your hair so you have two choices:
a) Shave all your hair off.
b) Get rid of your owner.
I know it's a very difficult decision – and you'll want to think long and hard about it.
P.S. Don't forget to write to WOOF! when you're looking for a new house for your owner to live in.

Dear Dr Rex

My master doesn't like me burying bones in the garden. How can I change his mind?

Digger, Dorking

Dear Digger,
Start burying them in the living room instead.

Dear Dr Rex

Up until now I have been my master's only pet but now he wants to buy a goat. I am very worried about the smell.

Sniffer, Surrey

Dear Sniffer,
Don't worry – If you've managed to put up with your master's smell for this long, I'm sure the goat will be able to, as well.

Dear Dr Rex

You know how they say that after a while dogs start to become like their owners? Well, my mistress is a TV newsreader and I am worried I'm getting like her. What can I do?

Square Eyes, Southampton

Dear Square Eyes,
I don't quite understand your problem ... can you give me the main points again?

Pet Owner PROBLEMS

Dear Dr Rex

I'm a young pup who hasn't got an owner. Every day the same man comes to see me in the pet shop. He says he's thinking of buying me because his own dog is too busy to fetch his slippers and go for walks. I'm worried because his house, 25 Medical Gardens, sounds like a really boring place to live.

Puppy, PetWorld

Dear Puppy,
I'm sure it's a very nice place ... hang on! 25 Medical Gardens? That's where I live!!!

EDITOR'S NOTE: No time for any more letters this issue. Dr Rex has had to rush home suddenly to see a man about some slippers.

When you go to fetch the paper from the newsagent does your owner grab it from you before you get the chance to read it? Never mind – now you can order some books to really get your teeth into with WOOF!'s own

BOW WOW

The Sausages of Paris

by Francis Bacon

Big Dangerous Dogs

by Al Satian

Small Annoying Dogs

by P. K. Nese

BOOKCLUB

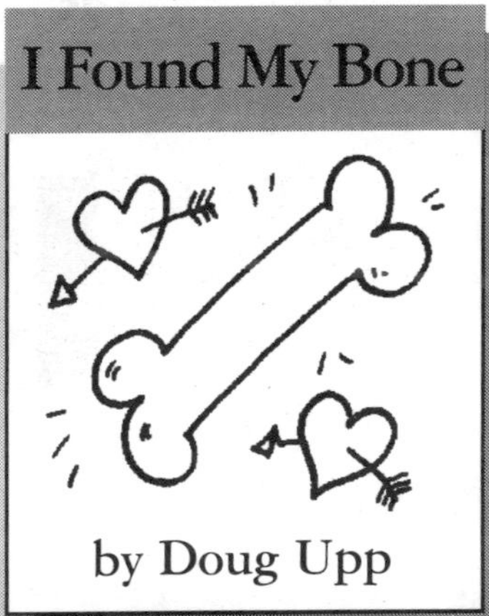

Special Offer!

Order any of these books and get *Old Mother Hubbard's Cookery Book* Free*

* We can afford to give it away free because the pages are all bare.

TRAVEL SECTION

Wish You

My great grandfather was a coyote and I can still howl at the moon. Especially when I get too close to a cactus!

USA

Sausages are a very common food over here.

Germany

Or at least they were common before I scoffed them all.

Beware! This must be the only country in the world where the postman tries to bite YOU!

Transylvania

Were Hair ...

Why waste time on the same boring old 'walkies' every night of the week? WOOF's travel reporter Bernard St Bernard has sent back these postcards from the top tourist spots for hounds on holiday.

You can find really nice patterned leashes here, although they may be a little tight. Especially if you've mistakenly picked up a boa constrictor.

Amazon Jungle

The weather here is beautiful and sunny all day long ... which is all very well if you've got a fur coat that actually comes OFF!

Spain

TRAVEL SECTION

SIRLOIN SLIPPERS

Are you tired of having to fetch your owner's smelly old slippers every evening?

Get your owner to buy a pair of new **SIRLOIN SLIPPERS**, *specially sprayed with beef essence so that every trip from the bedroom means a meaty mouthful for you.*

SIRLOIN SLIPPERS *are guaranteed to provide complete comfort.**

(Especially for us. If your owner has to buy a new pair every time you accidentally eat the old ones, we'll be very comfortably off indeed!)*

News Round-up

Monstrous Mother Munches Meaty Mouthful

She may have gone to the cupboard to get her poor doggy a bone, but police have now discovered that the cupboard was not bare when she got there. In fact Mother Hubbard was seen scoffing the bone herself. The witnesses were all children of her neighbour, the Old Lady who Lives in a Shoe. Mother Hubbard says once she gets out of prison she's definitely going to give her the boot.

Canine Crushed in Cow Crash

A little dog has been squashed by a cow in a tragic accident following the first ever attempt at non-stop jumping-over-the-moon. 'Serves him right for standing there laughing instead of getting out of my way,' said the cow angrily. (A cat was also hurt in the incident ... so it's not all bad news.)

Scientists Scratch Sleepy Scheme

Scientists have abandoned a ten-year project costing $500,000 aimed at discovering whether or not dogs dream. 'It's been a complete waste of money,' said Doctor S. Nooze yesterday. 'We've spent the last ten years carefully writing down everything this stupid mutt is supposed to have dreamt about while he was lying there snoring ... and now we've dis-

Speedy's Sporting Scandal

Speedy Sam, the world champion greyhound, was last night disqualified from the sport in a shock decision by racetrack judges. 'It's not fair,' said Sam. 'I finished the race long before any of the other dogs.' 'We know,' said the judges. 'But that's because none of the other dogs were on roller skates.'

overed that he made the vhole thing up.'

Ve at WOOF! think it's good idea to close the xperiment down – after ll, isn't it much better to et sleeping dogs lie?

Mutt's Mischief in Meadow

A dog has just been charged with worrying sheep. He told them he'd read in WOOF! that wool was going out of fashion.

Zany Zebra Zooms through Zoo

Yes, we know this has nothing to do with dogs ... but we couldn't find a dog beginning with 'z' to complete the headline.

Another......

We know lots of loyal WOOF! readers get absolutely sick of those stupid 'Beware of the Dog' signs that owners insist on sticking on their front door. After all, everyone admits that dogs are the sweetest and most gentle of creatures (and if they don't admit it, we'll bite them!). So instead, here are some really useful signs to cut out and stick around your house.

Beware of the Bog

For houses with whiffy toilets.

Beware of The Snog

For houses with aunties who come to visit.

Beware of the POG

For houses where owners play silly games all the time.

SIGN Mess

Beware of The Hog

For houses where your owner eats more than you do.

Beware of The Clog

For houses where owners like dancing a lot.

Beware of The Sprog

For houses with naughty toddlers.

Beware of the ickle cutey fluffy bunny

Yes, WE know you're not a ickle cutey fluffy bunny ... but the POSTIE doesn't!

Never able to dig up something delicious when you want to?

IT'S TIME YOU GOT YOURSELF A BRAND NEW

MOBILE BONE!

- **Works anywhere in the world**
- **Small and easy to carry***

*(Especially when you've chewed it up into little bits.)

To order your own MOBILE BONE, call us today. (And if we won't give you one, please don't bite our ears off.)

Here they come! The Hunkiest Hounds in the Music Biz...

RUFF!

Yes, RUFF! have got all the ingredients to make them the latest pop supergroup ... hairy chests, whiney voices and they've each got two left feet. But WOOF! is the first magazine to bring you this exclusive introduction to each of the dishy, doggy dudes in RUFF! We can hear you panting already. (Of course, if you're a dog, you probably pant most of the time anyway.)

MC FIDO

is famous for his unusual hairstyle, although how he gets it to stand on end like that is his best kept secret. MC Fido is the group's chief rapper. Unfortunately, like all dogs he's not very good at spelling and got 'rapper' mixed up with 'wrapper'. If YOU've ever tried to wrap your tongue around a live microphone, you won't have too much trouble getting your hair to stand on end either.

AL

is short for Alsatian. Even though he's the fittest member of the group, he's the one who gets the least fan mail. He's very keen on working out and enjoys long runs in the early morning.
He particularly likes running after the postman, which might explain why he has that problem with fan mail ...

FLASH

gets his name because he's one of the most dazzling dancers in the whole of showbiz. No RUFF! concert is complete without him doing backflips, turning somersaults and jumping from one end of the stage to the other. Is the secret of his success natural talent or constant practice? 'Neither – it's because the other two are such rotten dancers, they keep stepping on my tail!'

STOP PRESS! Just as we were finishing this article, it was announced that RUFF! have split up so that the three band members can follow solo careers. Music lovers all over the country are reported to be in tears. (And we don't blame them – now there'll be three times as many horrible records to listen to!)

WOOF!

LIVE AND EXCLUSIVE SONG LYRICS

Get ready to rock, readers – over the page you'll find the words to all the songs on

RUFF's

LAST

CD!

WELL, OF COURSE IT'S A BLANK PAGE, DUDES... DON'T YOU KNOW DOGGY MUSIC IS MUCH TOO HIGH PITCHED FOR HUMAN EARS TO HEAR...

THE DYNAMIC DOGGY DIET

Why be a pudgy pooch when you can be a hunky hound? Try out WOOF!'s doggy diet for a week and you'll never have to worry about your weight again.

Breakfast

The most important meal of the day, so don't miss out. Scoff at least twelve big juicy sausages.

Lunch

If you get peckish during the day you could ruin your whole diet. Best to have a couple of large pork chops and a large bowl of mince about now.

Dinner

Well, it's been a long hard day of dieting and as it's not good to overdo things, treat yourself to a large economy size tin of dogfood or three.

Simply follow this diet for a week and then weigh yourself ... See? Once you've broken the scales you'll never have to worry about your weight again!

HAPPY EATING!

YOU TOO CAN HAVE A BODY LIKE MINE...
IF YOU'RE NOT REALLY, REALLY CAREFUL!
ARRGH! IT'S GOING TO BE A LONG "WEIGHT" BEFORE I'M IN WORKING ORDER AGAIN!!

DOGGY DIY

SNEAKY STICK

Are you sick of having to run and fetch sticks for your owner all the time? Here's a simple way to make sure all that wretched fetching is a thing of the past.

1. Take an ordinary stick, just like the ones you are always being sent to fetch.

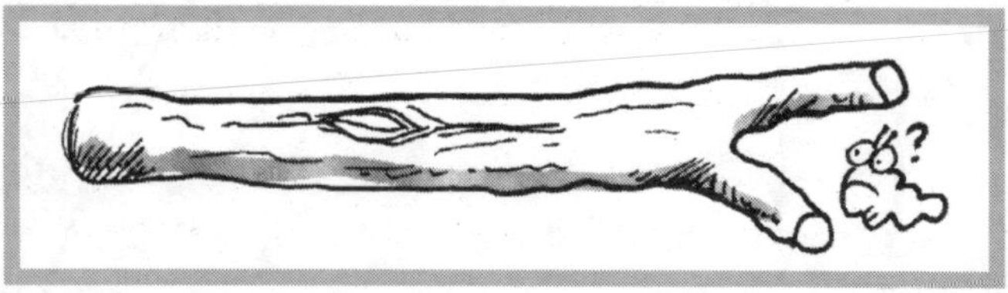

2. Get a piece of elastic, the longer the better, and nail one end of it to the stick. (Mind your paws.)

3. When your owner is about to throw the stick, place one paw on the end of the elastic.

4. SNAP! The stick will come back all by itself. (Sadly your owner's teeth may not come back all by themselves.)

FEARSOME FLAP

What better way for a cat to escape from doggy doom than through a handy cat flap? But this is no ordinary cat flap ... it's one you've very artistically painted on the front door. SPLATT!! Now the cat really is on the mat!

Patience

Your No. 1 animal agony aunt answers your queries

Dear Patience
I've been feeling bit itchy lately and I'm afraid I might have fleas. What should I do?
Scratchy, Sunderland

Dear Scratchy
Stop writing to me immediately. I don't want any of your horrid fleas jumping out of the envelope.

Dear Patience
I'm a bulldog and I'm worried that my face is a bit ugly. What can I do?
Pugsly, Peckham

Dear Pugsly
Stop worrying – compared to me, ALL other dogs are ugly. (And not nearly as modest either.)

Poodle

Dear Patience
I'm an old dog and I just can't seem to learn any new tricks. Can you help?
Scruffy, Southampton

Dear Scruffy
Here's a trick for you – try disappearing off my nice clean problem page. I can do without scruffy animals like you! At least my next writer bothered to use scented notepaper ...

Dear Patience
You've got to help me, my silly owner keeps insisting I have a bath. I've managed to avoid him for three months but he's closing in fast.
Whiffy, Woking

Dear Whiffy
ARRGH! So that's why your notepaper is scented! Someone throw a bucket of water over this dog RIGHT NOW!

Patience Poodle

Dear Patience
I'm confused. I know dogs aren't supposed to like cats, but I think they're quite cute actually.
Cuddles, Clapham

Dear Cuddles
Really! I know most dogs who write to me are sad, smelly losers but even THEY know that cats and dogs are never supposed to mix.

Dear Patience
Actually, that's where you're wrong. Since we've had to put up with reading **YOUR** stuck-up rubbish we've decided that cats aren't so bad after all. Now get lost, we're off to share a nice big bowl of cream.
Scratchy, Pugsly, Scruffy, Whiffy, Cuddles and every other WOOF! reader.

I've got beautiful clear skin with not a spot in sight – which is a real disaster considering

I'm a Dalmatian!!

That's why I use

SIMPSON'S SPOT CREAM

It doesn't take more than 101 dabs to make me the blotchiest bow-wow in town.

Remember the name: Simpson's Spot Cream

It's black and white and spread all over

SPORTS FACT FILE

Name: 'Tiger'

Sport: Football

What's your position?
On the sideline – I'm Ramshackle Rovers' Team Mascot.
When did you get your first taste of football success?
When I bit Ramshackle Rovers' talent scout.
Did your team always have a dog as a mascot?
No, they used to have a cat, but it ... ahem ... disappeared.
How good is your goalkeeper at saving?
Well, he wasn't very successful at saving the cat ...
What do the crowd sing whenever you're on the pitch?
'Hair we go, Hair we go, Hair we go ...'
What's your biggest ambition?
To play in the World Pup Final.
We hear you've been banned from Ramshackle Rovers' ground for the next couple of games. Why is that?
The pitch is waterlogged.
What's that got to do with you?
Goalpost, lamp post ... they all look the same to me!

Name: 'Flash'

Sport: Greyhound Racing

When did you first start running?
When I was a pup. There were six of us, and only five tins of dog food.

When did you get your first taste of racing success?
When I bit a greyhound racing talent scout. He was very upset – he'd left his last job at Ramshackle Rovers' football club because of a very similar incident.

What shampoo do you use on your coat?
Wash and Ready, Set, Go ...

Why are you called 'Flash'?
Because I'd feel very stupid if I was called 'Persil Automatic'.

Why do you like chasing the electronic hare?
I don't know – I just get a real charge out of it.

What do the crowd sing when you're running up the track?
'Hare we go, Hare we go, Hare we go ...'

Are you as fast as your name suggests?
I certainly am! In the last World Championship Race I was going at 60 kilometres per hour.

So how come you're not world champion?
Unfortunately, I was going in the wrong direction ...

BARK TO THE FUTURE!

WOOF! looks into the canine crystal ball to see whether it will still be a dog's life in tomorrow's world ...

TODAY: You have to dig big holes to bury your bones.
TOMORROW: A special shrinking ray will make the bones smaller.

TODAY: You chase cars.
TOMORROW: You'll chase spaceships ... so you'd better get in some running practice.

TODAY: You tire your owner out during walkies.
TOMORROW: You're the tired one. Your owner's got twenty-two legs!

TODAY: You make lamp posts rusty.
TOMORROW: You'll need to check that the 'lamp post' isn't actually a super-thin robot from the planet ZZARG.

TODAY: You chase the postie.
TOMORROW: The Alien postie chases YOU!

TODAY:
You sometimes don't do what you're told.
TOMORROW:
Some things NEVER change.

TV Guide

TOP TAIL-O-VISION! Your guide to the week's top pooch programmes.

Sunday

10am Morning Service
In this programme, the vicar really does wear a dog collar!

9pm London's Barking
The exciting programme about a poodle who joins the fire brigade. So gripping you'll probably forget to have supper, but don't worry – every episode features a hot dog.

Monday

9am Breakfast News

1pm Lunchtime News

6pm Evening News
(We need the evening news, because by then dogs will have forgotten what they had for lunch and breakfast.)

8pm Paw-lice Report
You can help your friendly neighbourhood police dogs track down real-life criminals. We'd tell you more about the show only one of the real-life criminals nicked our video.

Tuesday

7.30pm Home and Away with the Neighbours of Brookenders Street
This may be the most boring soap on television, but it's very popular with us doggies ... especially since we discovered that our owners would rather take us for a walk in the pouring rain than watch it.

Wednesday

4pm Dog-prah
The popular chat show where dogs come along and talk about their problems. (One of the problems being that dogs aren't actually able to talk.)

8pm World of Wildlife
The programme that takes a weekly look at some of the world's wildest and most fearsome creatures. This week: your owner's two-year-old niece and nephew who come round every weekend to pull your ears

The thrill of the chase in Wednesday's 'World of Wildlife'.

and tweak your tail.

Thursday

8pm Top of the Pups
All the latest chart-topping hits and lots of dogs dancing. (They have to keep dancing because there aren't any trees or lamp posts in a television studio.)

Friday

We're not listing any programmes today ... if you watched them you might miss tonight's dog food commercial.

Saturday

8pm National Lottery Draw
Yes, we know dogs aren't allowed to buy lottery tickets, but watch this with your owner in case this is the week they get a big surprise. (In fact, you can guarantee they'll get a big surprise if their numbers come up and you've chewed up their ticket!)

WOOF! ADVERTISEMENTS

IF YOU'RE A MONGREL WITH A MESSAGE, THIS IS THE SECTION FOR YOU!

Forgetful Owner seeks Retriever. Must be good at finding things. Contact me at ... oh no! I've forgotten the address.

Bloodhound wanted. Must like long walks at night and be able to put up with owner being a pain in the neck.
Contact D. Racula, Transylvania.

Burglar seeks dog to act as lookout. Must be good at sneaking around. No Dalmatians, please – they're always spotted.

Dog wanted by butcher. I've already had two thousand replies to this ad, but listen, you mangy mutts: I don't want just any dog – I want the one that swiped fifty pounds' worth of sausages from my shop last week!

Pekinese wanted. Also seeking Peki-hands and Peki-boomps-a-daisy.

Vet wanted. Must be good at treating indigestion. Contact the dog that swiped fifty pounds' worth of sausages from the butcher last week.

Forgetful Owner seeks Retriever. OOPS! Didn't I already put this ad in the magazine?

St Bernard seeks Owner. (No, not a new owner, my old owner – I think I lost him in a snowdrift somewhere.)

WOOF! reader seeks dog with no teeth. The dog I have now keeps biting pages out of my

Mu
at...

Blo
wal
a p
Tra

Bu
loo
arou
alw

Do
had
liste
any
pou
last

he dog of your choice.
know that's probably you,
ut call us anyway.)

D-A-SAUSAGE

you make both ends meat.

SPOT THE BALL Competiton

Here's another in WOOF!'s exciting series of *Spot the Ball* competitions. This time, we've used a photograph taken during the latest game featuring Tiger, the famous team mascot of Ramshackle Rovers and star of WOOF!'s Sports Factfile.

Simply place an 'X' where you think the ball in this picture might be and you could win a year's supply of dog food. (If you're having difficulty, there's a clue at the bottom of the page.)

SEND-A-SAUSAGE

CLUE: The ball in this picture is actually *inside* Tiger, famous team mascot of Ramshackle Rovers. Don't worry, you wouldn't have won the dog food anyway, because he's scoffed that, too.

Roses are red, violets are blue, Who needs flowers when a SAUSAGE will do?

No more worries about what to give the dog of your dreams! Simply dial SEND-A-SAUSAGE and we'll deliver a prime banger to the dog of your choice. (Yes, we know that's probably you, but call us anyway.)

SEND-A-SAUSAGE

We'll help you make both ends meat.

Are you a top dog?

Are you a perfect pooch or a doggy disgrace? Try our Clever Canine Quiz and find out!

1 ***When your owner throws you a stick, you:***

a) run and fetch it because you love getting all hot and bothered.
b) run and fetch it because you hate getting hot and bothered but you love your owner.
c) stay where you are because you love watching your owner get all hot and bothered.

2 ***What's your favourite trick?***

a) Balancing a ball on your nose.
b) Balancing a rubber bone on your nose.
c) Turning up your nose at the whole idea of doing tricks.

3 ***Do you chase the postman***

a) every morning?
b) every second morning?
c) Who wants to get up that early? You'd rather send him a letter with a picture of your teeth.

4 When it's time for walkies, you most enjoy:

a) taking a long walk round the park.
b) taking a short walk down the street.
c) watching your owner walk round the house looking for you, while you hide under the bed.

5 Are you a good watch dog?

a) Yes, I'm always ready for trouble.
b) Yes, I always stay alert.
c) Sorry – I dozed off and didn't hear the question.

6 Do you like cats?

a) No.
b) No.
c) No. (Got the message, yet?)

7 How many times a day do you eat?

a) Four or five times.
b) Seven or eight times.
c) Can't answer the question – it's rude to talk with your mouth full.

Scoring: If your answers were mostly Cs, you're obviously one of the fattest, laziest, greediest animals around. If your answers were mostly As or Bs don't worry – just keep reading WOOF! and you'll learn to behave like a proper dog in no time!

GRR-sery Rhymes!

Fancy having to scrape about in bare cupboards just to find a measly bone! It's no laughing matter the way we dogs get treated in nursery rhymes. We've had hundreds of letters from WOOF! readers demanding equal rhyming rights. Now here are some nursery rhymes rewritten to show a definite doggy difference.

Mary had a great
big dog,
Much better than
a lamb.
'Cos when she brought
her dog to school,
The teachers all
would scram.

Little Bo Peep has lost her sheep,
And doesn't know where to find them.

Good ... serves her right for
sacking her sheepdog.

Humpty Dogty
Sat on the wall.
Humpty Dogty
Started to bawl.
All the king's horses and all the king's men
Left the country and were never seen again.

Little Miss Muffet sat
on a tuffet,
Eating her curds
and whey,
Along came a spider
and sat down
beside her,
And her Rottweiler said
'Go on – Make My Day.'

Sing a song of sixpence,
A pocketful of rye.
Four and Twenty Labradors
Baked in a pie.
Before the pie was cooked,
A bell began to ring.
The RSPCA had come to take away the king.

It's TOP of the PUPs!

WOOF!'s REGULAR LOOK AT WHAT'S HOT AND WHAT'S NOT IN THE CANINE CHARTS.

1 **'You Ain't Nothin' But A Hound Dog'** Elvis Presley

2 **'You Need Your Eyes Tested'** Elvis Presley's Cat

3 **'Theme From 101 Dalmatians'** Original Artists

4 **'Theme From 101 Dalmatians'** The rest of the Original Artists (There are far too many Dalmatians to fit on one CD.)

5 **'How Much Is That Doggy in the Window?'** The Pet Shop Boys

6 **'No, Really How Much Is That Doggy in the Window?'** The Pet Shop Adults (They took so long deciding on a price, the band grew up in the meantime.)

7 **'Born Free'** The Pet Shop Dogs (Oh, and the dogs escaped from the pet shop while the band were growing up.)

8 **'Saturday Daytime Fever'** Original Soundtrack (Well, you wouldn't send a dog out on a night like this.)

9 **'I've Just Been Let Out Of The Dog Pound'** (We don't know who the singer is, but it's definitely a new release.)

10 **This Year's Eurovision Entry** (Well, everyone says the music's gone to the dogs ...)

SPECiAL TRUE LiFE REPORT

In the next few pages WOOF! brings you the gripping true-life story of one of the most fearless, rugged dogs in the world. Yes, our rover-ing reporter braved ice and biting winds to get the first ever in-depth exclusive interview with the

CANADIAN HUSKY

SORRY, READERS... ALL THAT ICE AND BITING WIND HAS MADE HIM TOO HUSKY TO DO THE INTERVIEW... HE'S WRAPPED UP WITH A NICE HOT CUP OF COCOA INSTEAD!

NEXT ISSUE: WOOF! interviews the totally savage Fighting Pit Bull terriers of Shanghai (unless they have to go to their embroidery class).

Celebrity PROFILE

Youv'e seen her swim across raging rivers ... or at least you WOULD have seen all these things if dogs were allowed into the cinema. Join us now as we spend a day with that top action hero

LUVVIE the wonder dog!

5 AM

Luvvie has to get up very early to be on the movie set. (Mind you, it's not too difficult to wake up when you share your doggy basket with three security guards.)

6 AM

Luvvie spends an hour having her face made up and her hair done (of course when you're a dog, having your face made up and your hair done are one and the same thing!).

Luvvie grabs a last chance to go over some of her lines.

At last Luvvie shoots her first big scene in which she catches a stick.

Luvvie takes her lunch break and takes time out to give autographs to lucky fans.

This afternoon we're filming one of the action scenes. Don't worry, Luvvie fans – her place will be taken by a cleverly disguised stunt dog.

Like all big stars, Luvvie takes a big interest in her movies from start to finish.

Luvvie's chauffeur-driven limousine arrives at the end of a long hard day. (No, you fool, of course she doesn't ride in it – she just chases it all the way home.)

Be a REAL Watchdog ...
Treat yourself to this beautiful new

ROVERDEX

The timepiece for classy canines.
Why not buy one for each paw?

ROVERDEX

For the dog of distinction

(Also for the dog with the owner who's dumb enough to pay £1,600,000.99.)

DOG'S

Every week our roving reporter rates a number of top restaurants ... (or at least snuffles around the bins by the kitchen door).

YUM YUM!

Worth wagging your tail for

Only come here if you need walkies

YUK!

Red Dragon Chinese Restaurant

I didn't get a chance to eat any food here – every time the chef tried to throw away the old chop sticks I couldn't stop myself fetching them back.

Rating:

dinners

McBurgers Fast Food Bar
I know why this is called a fast food bar – I had to move really fast when this big, bad-tempered clown caught me going through the bins.

Rating: 

Patel's Curry House
I don't mind the fact that what I thought were little red sausages turned out to be little red CHILLI PEPPERS. But I don't think there was any need for the kitchen staff to sing 'How much is that doggy in the Vindaloo?'. Now this doggy diner is really hot under the collar.

Rating: 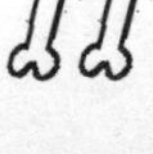

Luigi's Pizza Parlour
I've always wanted to try eating spaghetti in the style of that romantic scene from *Lady and the Tramp.* Unfortunately, I got a bit too carried away with the spaghetti. When my girlfriend finally unwraps herself it's going to be more like *'Lady and the Trampled'*.

Rating: 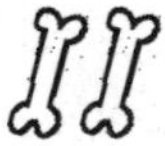

TAILS OUT OF

Were you a top pooch pupil or bottom of the canine class? WOOF! looks into the lives of dogs and their celebrity owners with these top secret reports from obedience school.

ADAM'S ACADEMY
FOR COURTEOUS CANINES

Dog Owner Dr Frankenstein

Marks 4/10

Comments: No longer a complete monster but often acts like a nut and bolts.

ADAM'S ACADEMY
FOR COURTEOUS CANINES

Dog Owner Genie of the Lamp

Marks 2/10

Comments: Easily rubbed up the wrong way.

ADAM'S ACADEMY
FOR COURTEOUS CANINES

Dog Owner Dr Dolittle

Marks 8/10

Comments: Talks back in class.

SCHOOL

ADAM'S ACADEMY

FOR COURTEOUS CANINES

Dog Owner David Copperfield 'Magician'

Marks 2/10

Comments: Very hard to teach him any new tricks.

TAILS OUT OF SCHOOL

ADAM'S ACADEMY
FOR COURTEOUS CANINES

Dog Owner Houdini

Marks 9/10

Comments: Keeps escaping from his leash.

ADAM'S ACADEMY
FOR COURTEOUS CANINES

Dog Owner The Invisible Man

Marks 7/10

Comments: Hard to see any improvement.

ADAM'S ACADEMY
FOR COURTEOUS CANINES

Dog Owner Flea circus owner

Marks 2/10

Comments: Needs to start the whole class again from scratch.

You know the feeling. It's late, you're hungry and you're looking forward to digging up that big juicy bone you buried two weeks ago ... but some other dirty dog has got there first!

Make no bones about it – now there's a better way to guard your grub.

Deposit your doggy treasures in

BONEBANK

No more worrying about where you're going to dig up tonight's dinner.
You can be sure your precious bones are being guarded 24 hours a day by our team of hungry Dobermans. (Don't worry about your bones, though – they may be hungry but they're also vegetarian!)

BONEBANK

Call us on the tele-bone today.

0800 B-I-G B-O-N-E

POOCH POSERS

If you were a human what job would you have?

1. Dave Dachshund
I reckon I'd be a really good shoe salesman. Let's face it, when all you see all day are people's shoes, you become a bit of an expert.

2. Derek Dalmatian
I'd be a famous artist. I know I can't draw very well but who needs to when you can simply join up your own dots?

3. Bernard Bloodhound

I'm sick of solving crimes and having my handler get all the credit. I'd be a policeman myself – then they'd see my achievements are *not* to be sniffed at.

4. Darlene Doberman

I'd join the postal service. Yes, I know I chase postmen every day. But imagine how much more fun I could have if I was hiding among them!

5. Pauline Poodle

Me, be a smelly, ugly human ... are you joking? I'll have to book another trip to the beauty parlour immediately – just the thought's made my fur stand on end!

Dog-gone

YES, IT'S ANOTHER PUP-ULAR PAGEFUL OF

What do you call a bloodhound with a cold?

A police sniffer dog.

What do dogs do when they can't find something?

Why did the human cross the road?

What's the world's fastest dog?

Because his dog dragged him – that'll teach him to hold the leash so tightly!

Why did the cat cross the road?

Because the dog was too slow starting up the steam-roller.

Will humans find any of these jokes funny?

ABSOLUTELY ARF-FUL JOKES ...

Werewoofs.

How do you start a scruffy greyhound race?

Put an ad in WOOF!'s Lost and Hound section.

One, two, flea ... Go!

he dash-hound.

First Dog: I say, I say, my master's got no nose.

Second Dog: How does he smell?

First Dog: Terrible.

Second Dog: That's a very old joke.

First Dog: That's OK – I've got a very old master.

No – but they'll certainly make their dogs howl.

MEDAL ABOUT!

Ever wish you had a really INTERESTING owner? Well, now you ca pretend with WOOF!'s exclusive cut-out identity disc collection. 'Disc' could be your big break!

This dog belongs to
Superman
(So it's not a bird or a plane.)

This dog belongs to
Darth Vader
(But don't breathe a word.)

This dog belongs
ET
(Please give it som
money to phone hom

This dog belongs to
Tarzan
(So don't monkey around.)

THIS DOG BELONGS TO
JAMES BOND
(But keep it a secret.)

This dog belongs to
Arnold Schwarzenegger
(But he'll be back!)

This dog belongs to
Batman
(Please give it some dinner, dinner, dinner.)

This dog belongs to

(Fill in the name of your choice here.)

STOP PRESS!

If you enjoyed WOOF!, here's a pet publication you really WON'T like ...

Believe it or not, those dirty dogs at Puffin have agreed to let those horrible cat creatures have a Mad Mag all to their smelly selves.

Rumour has it that the creepy kitties have been secretly studying WOOF!, trying to produce a Mad Mag that's faster, furrier and even funnier. PURR! is full of Fearsome Feline Features, Monstrous Moggie Mirth, and as for the adverts ... well, we've come out in an allergic reaction already!

*** WARNING: If you DO enjoy PURR! and then find yourself wanting to curl up with a ball of wool and a nice cool bowl of milk, re-read this issue of WOOF! immediately! That's going too dog-gone far!**